T0268227

The Jungle

The Jungle

Anthony MacMahon
Thomas McKechnie

PLAYWRIGHTS CANADA PRESS
TORONTO

Jacket design by Adrian Morningstar
Author photo of Anthony MacMahon © Eleni Katsuras
Author photo of Thomas McKechnie © Graham Isador

Playwrights Canada Press
202-269 Richmond St. W., Toronto, ON M5V 1X1
416.703.0013 | info@playwrightscanada.com | www.playwrightscanada.com

For professional or amateur production rights, please contact Playwrights Canada Press.

LIBRARY AND ARCHIVES CANADA CATALOGUING IN PUBLICATION
Title: The jungle / Anthony MacMahon and Thomas McKechnie.
Names: MacMahon, Anthony, author. | McKechnie, Thomas, author.
Description: A play.
Identifiers: Canadiana (print) 20230224806 | Canadiana (ebook) 20230224849
  | ISBN 9780369104403 (softcover) | ISBN 9780369104427 (EPUB)
  | ISBN 9780369104410 (PDF)
Classification: LCC PS8625.M35 J86 2023 | DDC C812/.6—dc23

Playwrights Canada Press operates on land which is the ancestral home of the
Anishinaabe Nations (Ojibwe / Chippewa, Odawa, Potawatomi, Algonquin, Saulteaux,
Nipissing, and Mississauga), the Wendat, and the members of the Haudenosaunee
Confederacy (Mohawk, Oneida, Onondaga, Cayuga, Seneca, and Tuscarora), as well as
Metis and Inuit peoples. It always was and always will be Indigenous land.

We acknowledge the financial support of the Canada Council for the Arts, the
Ontario Arts Council (OAC), Ontario Creates, and the Government of Canada for
our publishing activities.

Canada Council
for the Arts
Conseil des arts
du Canada

ONTARIO ARTS COUNCIL
CONSEIL DES ARTS DE L'ONTARIO
an Ontario government agency
un organisme du gouvernement de l'Ontario

ONTARIO | ONTARIO
CREATES | CRÉATIF

To our mothers

Foreword

By Guillermo Verdecchia

I had the good fortune to direct the premiere of *The Jungle* in Toronto at the Tarragon Theatre, and though I had no doubt it was a very good play, I was struck by how intently, anxiously even, people—especially those in their twenties and early thirties—followed the play. The drama in *The Jungle* is, in a sense, pretty low-key. Will Jack and Veronyka make rent? Will Jack go back to school? Will Veronyka become a butcher? Who'd have thought this late capitalist love story punctuated by explications of basic Marxist economics would be so compelling? (Anthony MacMahon and Thomas McKechnie, that's who: Canada's foremost anarcho-communist-activist-civil-servant playwriting duo.)

At the centre of play is the story of an early twenty-first century precariat couple (she's an economic migrant from Moldova; he is a Chinese Canadian economics student taxi driver) who meet and fall in love—or do they?—marry, and struggle to, as they themselves put it, "get ahead."

Seems simple enough.

But what does "get ahead" mean? What are we getting ahead *of* when we "get ahead"? (If Jack and Veronyka get ahead, does that mean someone else is left behind? Can everybody get ahead?) *The Jungle* stages this struggle to "get ahead," and, in doing so, reveals the mechanism obscured by this innocuous-sounding phrase. Getting ahead for Jack and Veronyka means trying to extricate themselves from a structure designed to extract *value* from them.[1] In concretizing that structure, *The Jungle* does something few Canadian plays do—or even attempt. It looks beyond the individual to the structural.[2]

And there I think is the reason for all those hyper-focused audience members riveted by the everyday struggle of our protagonists: they glimpsed, perhaps, that their precarity was not necessarily their fault, not an individual failing, but a fundamental aspect of the structure they too live within.

The Jungle is a splendid, articulate rebuke to the glory-hallelujah capitalist praise songs that still ring out all around us, insisting that the so-called free market is the driver of wealth and prosperity, that economic "freedom" and political freedom go hand in hand, that rising profits result from increased efficiency and entrepreneurial risk-taking, that work is the best way out of poverty, and, finally, that, well, there aren't alternatives to capitalism anyway[3] so just . . . you know . . . shuddup already. The play compels because it stages what so many—again, especially young folk—are living today. But the play doesn't simply rehearse a certain experience, it also probes the gap between the aspirational world presented to us ("Condo after condo. Lights in the windows. People in the lights. Lives in the people. That's going to be us.") and the reality of our lives. And there lies its lefty and theatrical nous.

Not lessons in how to think correctly about economics, the capsule lectures refract that lived experience and become invitations to look again at our situation, to look differently. Those interventions make our condition—as folks struggling to "get ahead"—*strange*: not the way things are and always will be, but an invention, a construction, something that could be changed.

---

1 "[Capital] has resolved personal worth into exchange value." Engels and Marx, *The Communist Manifesto.*
2 North American dramaturgy seems to me just as fixated on the individual as neoclassical economics.
3 An attitude Mark Fisher called Capitalist Realism.

There's more, much more, including the sheer narrative pleasure of play. And it's all expressed with more intelligence, humour, and compassion than I can muster here, which is hardly surprising given the outsize talent, brains, and hearts of its authors. So, let's turn without delay to the urgent, necessary play MacMahon and McKechnie have crafted for us.

Guillermo Verdecchia is a writer of drama, fiction, and film; a director, dramaturge, actor, and translator whose work has been seen and heard on stages, screens, and radios across the country and around the globe. He is a recipient of the Governor General's Literary Award for Drama, a four-time winner of the Chalmers Canadian Play Award, a recipient of Dora and Jessie Awards, and sundry film festival awards. He lives in Toronto with Tamsin Kelsey, his partner of many years, and their two dachshunds.

The Jungle was first produced by Tarragon Theatre, Toronto, in their Extraspace from October 1 to November 3, 2019, with the follow cast and creative team:

Veronyka: Shannon Currie
Jack: Matthew Gin

Director: Guillermo Verdecchia
Set and Costume Design: Shannon Lea Doyle
Lighting Design: Michelle Ramsay
Apprentice Director: Alice Lundy
Dialect Coach: Diane Pitblado
Stage Manager: Kathleen Jones

Characters

Veronyka
Jack

Notes

Ellipses in brackets (. . .) indicate a short non-verbal interjection. For example, sucking of teeth, a mouth click, a tongue snap, etc.

VERONYKA: The Tilted Kilt.

JACK: What's the nearest intersection?

VERONYKA: Yonge and the Esplanade.

JACK: Oh yeah, that place. I've picked up a lot of people from there.

VERONYKA: I imagine you have.

JACK: I've never been inside. Is it any good?

VERONYKA: It's definitely something.

JACK: I'll have to go sometime.

VERONYKA: You really don't.

JACK: Are you meeting friends there?

VERONYKA: No. I work there.

JACK: Two jobs.

Unless you live in that factory I just picked you up from.

I feel you. Done seven hours already today, got another nine more before I'm done. I'm surprised my butt hasn't fused to the seat yet.

If you want to rest, I won't drive like a moron.

It's Friday. Downtown bar, it'll be a long shift . . . I'm not a creep. That's what a creep would say.

What I mean is—

VERONYKA: That . . . that'd be nice. Thank you.

JACK: No problem.

I pause the meter for a few minutes while she sleeps. I know I shouldn't, but those long shifts. No one should have to work like this. I put the *Financial Times* podcast on low and try to drive carefully. It's like leisure time for me.

   A honk.

Shit. Sorry!

VERONYKA: *(checks her phone)* Сука блядь. *(Suka bliad.) [Son of a bitch.]*

JACK: What's wrong?

VERONYKA: My shift starts in five.

JACK: We should be there.

VERONYKA: But I—do you mind if I change in the car?

JACK: Umm . . .

VERONYKA: I really can't be late.

>   *She starts changing.*

JACK: Okay, yeah.

>   *JACK decides to not object, just stares really hard at the road.*

VERONYKA: Can you pull down that mirror? I need to check my hair.

JACK: Is that your uniform?

VERONYKA: They tip well.

JACK: *(arriving at the Kilt)* Here you go.

VERONYKA: Thanks for letting me sleep.

JACK: It's $44.50.

VERONYKA: That seems low.

JACK: I'm a good driver. Wait, take my card.

VERONYKA: I normally take Uber.

JACK: You didn't today. My dad says, "Regular customer, good customer. Good customer, discount."

VERONYKA: Thank you, uhh . . . Ding Hang?

JACK: Ding Heung is my dad's name. I'm Jack.

VERONYKA: Veronyka.

JACK: Don't work too hard, Veronyka.

VERONYKA: You too.

〰

JACK: Why can't Veronyka and Jack get ahead?

VERONYKA: The play just started. No one knows they can't get ahead yet.

JACK: Right. This play is about my character, Jack.

VERONYKA: And my character, Veronyka.

JACK: And about their . . . struggles. For love, for fulfillment, to come out on top.

VERONYKA: To understand why they struggle, you need to understand economics. Economics is not a hard science, it's a set of lenses. The orthodox lens is neoliberal, or neoclassical. However, given as this is an intelligent audience interested in a diversity of thought, let's look at a heterodox perspective— Marxist economics. In *Capital*, Marx says there are two forms of exchange—CMC and MCM. The CMC form is how workers like Jack and Veronyka use and exchange money.

VERONYKA writes on the board: commodity 1 to money to commodity 2, where the value of commodity 1 and 2 are equal, compared to money 1 to capital commodity to money 2, where the value of money 2 is greater than money 1.

JACK: Your labour is a commodity—commodity 1. You exchange it for money. You exchange that money to buy the commodities you need to survive—commodity 2. You work in a bread factory? You're making bread to earn bread to buy bread.

VERONYKA: The MCM form is how owners use and exchange money. They exchange money 1 to purchase a commodity (like labour and bread factories) to make more money (money 2) at the end of the exchange.

JACK: These two forms have one large difference. For workers there's no change in value—commodity 1 is equal to commodity 2. For owners there is a change in value—money 2 is greater than money 1. It is self-evident that there is no reason to have an amount of money, exchange it for a factory, and end the exchange with the same amount of money you began with. It simply wouldn't be worth the bother.

VERONYKA: This change from money 1 to money 2 goes by a lot of different names: profit, return on investment, growth. Marx calls it "surplus value." Where does the "surplus" come from?

JACK: We'll get back to that.

〰

VERONYKA: I don't believe his line about the fare being low because "he's a good driver" but if he wants to charge me less for the show I gave him, it's his choice.

Vlad shows up at the Kilt. He's my immigration guy, Canadian son of Russians. Nice suit, BMW, comes in from Mississauga. He got me to the factory as a "temporary foreign worker" and got me here under the table. I rent an apartment from his cousin. I pay him, to keep everything going smooth. He sits at the bar and smiles at me. He is always smiling.

I finish my shift. I could wait for a streetcar to take me back to Etobicoke. $3.25. $35. A cab ride home doesn't make sense.

She calls.

JACK: Hello?

VERONYKA: Hello.

JACK: And I pick her up.

VERONYKA: And he drives me home. Every week, Thursday, Friday, and Saturday nights.

JACK: She finishes her shift, I drive her home. That's as close as I get to a break.

VERONYKA: I don't think he ever charges me full price. Or even close.

JACK: Time is precious for her, and it's precious for me but that doesn't stop me. A long left turn. A slow acceleration off the lights. An extra moment at the stop sign. I steal seconds from us and give them back to us.

VERONYKA: I don't mind. We listen to his radio, his podcasts. He could talk for hours about politics, city planning, about economics. I complain about my bus route to the factory and he goes off about some politician filling in subway tunnels with concrete which I don't understand.

(to JACK) All this learning and you drive cab? Are you a student?

JACK: I dropped out two years ago.

VERONYKA: But he's going back soon. He has plan.

JACK: Why did you leave Moldova?

VERONYKA: Moldova is shit. And gets more shit every day.

JACK: Why?

VERONYKA: Bankers stole economy. In America they built a whole pyramid to take everyone's money. In Moldova they just took the money from our accounts and put in theirs. Much simpler. We had a friend who lived here, said there was money if I could fly over. That it was beautiful country full of good people who will help me. From here I can make as much money as a doctor does in Chişinău, send money home, and my brother Dmitri can go to university.

JACK: You like Canada?

VERONYKA shrugs, indifferent.

One night, as we pull up to her house, I put the cab in park. And she says good night, and I say good night. But she doesn't get out of the cab. She says:

VERONYKA: It was a good night.

JACK: She turns the keys and pulls them out of the ignition.

VERONYKA: Come inside.

JACK: And this happens.

VERONYKA: And this happens.

JACK: And this happens.

VERONYKA: We're both more tired than ever. One time, when we're having sex, he falls asleep. It's so sad, but so funny. I wake him up by laughing while I'm on top of him.

We can only meet Monday and Tuesday. They're slowest for cabs and restaurants.

JACK: Aba asks why revenue is down. I tell him it's Uber. He's still driving forty hours a week, he sees it. But he's suspicious. I've never lied to him about anything. I've never had anything worth lying about. I'm losing six hours a week though. I know it can't keep going.

VERONYKA: I drop three bottles of wine at work, my boss makes me pay for them. Customer price. $40 per bottle. Vlad comes to collect my weekly payment. I can only give him $200. "This isn't enough."

"There are other things girls like you can do for money. If you're having trouble keeping up with payment."

JACK: She stops responding to texts, she's cold on the phone when I call her.

Beat.

What are you doing tomorrow?

VERONYKA: I might take an extra shift. I need the money.

JACK: Oh . . .

VERONYKA: What?

JACK: . . . don't?

VERONYKA: I have to.

JACK: Spend the day with me. It's New Year's.

VERONYKA: It's February.

JACK: Chinese New Year's. My mom is going to make a hundred types of dumplings. My dad will get drunk and sing old communist songs.

VERONYKA: I need the money, Jack.

JACK: I know, but you've worked extra shifts this whole week and last week. Take a break.

VERONYKA: If I don't work I'm going to get deported.

JACK: That's crazy.

VERONYKA: My immigration guy. He told me if I don't increase his payments, he'll report me for working under the table.

JACK: Then you report him.

VERONYKA: He gets a fine, I get deported. I'm paying for my brother's school and my parents' everything right now. I can't do both and have days to myself. I'm sorry.

Beat.

JACK: Marry me.

VERONYKA: What?

JACK: You could marry me. I was born here, you could marry me and become a citizen. Then you can say fuck your immigration guy, you don't have to pay him anything. We can take days off and spend them together. You could meet my parents on Chinese New Year and tell them you're my fiancée.

VERONYKA: That's crazy.

JACK: People have gotten married for worse reasons. That's—that's not romantic.

VERONYKA: It kind of is.

JACK: Is that a yes?

She takes his hands.

We want to do it quickly. But different languages, different backgrounds, no shared living space—

VERONYKA: And Moldova has . . . bad record for these kind of marriages.

JACK: We can't raise any red flags. It has to be real.

VERONYKA: I want to keep wedding small, but Jack's parents want the whole community there. They're so happy for him.

JACK: Ba says he's looking forward to meeting Veronyka's parents.

VERONYKA: Fuck. The tickets would cost them a year's wages. "No, my grandma is sick, so my parents can't leave her."

JACK: He understands. He asks where to send the bill for their portion.

VERONYKA: I thought you said that the groom's parents pay for wedding in China.

JACK: Yeah, but the bride's parents pay for alcohol.

VERONYKA: Ba asks if my parents can afford to send money. What will Ma and Ba think when they find out? That I'm conning him. That I'm conning them.

JACK: Marius works for the government, and her parents have land. They can pay.

VERONYKA: My father processes park permits, and they have an allotment.

JACK: I say to give us the bill. It's almost $2,000. We empty out our savings and say it's from her parents.

VERONYKA: The night before the wedding Jack and I are brought to his mother's friends' apartment and there is a ceremony. They give us water infused with fruit and we bathe and change into new clothes. I receive my red marriage dress and my marriage shoes. I look like leading lady in an American movie set in China. They comb our hair and bless us in Chinese. When they run the comb through my hair I remember being a little girl and my grandmother combing my hair and braiding it and putting little flowers in it before church.

JACK: My cousin asks whether this is a green-card marriage or whether it's real. "It's a two-for-one."

VERONYKA: And suddenly it's the day. I only have a couple of guests. One of the girls from the Kilt is my maid of honour. I have to ask her how to spell her name so I could put it in the program. Jack's parents live in public housing and book out the party room. This dumpy little room covered in cheap Chinese decorations. My parents got married in Nativity Cathedral in Chişinău. A beautiful building, gold leaf on the wall and ceiling. A statue of Lenin in the square facing the church, watching the people rejoice. Outside party room there's a raccoon going through Tim Hortons garbage.

JACK appears.

JACK: Hey.

VERONYKA: Hey.

They step closer.

JACK: Hey.

VERONYKA: Hey.

Beat.

It's bad luck to see bride before wedding.

JACK: Only for white people.

Closer.

You're ... radiant.

VERONYKA: You're a little—

She fixes something on his suit.

There. Now you're perfect.

Her hand stays on him for a moment. She starts to withdraw it. He takes it.

JACK: Can we stay here? Can we skip the next part? Can we just stay in this little room together?

She kisses him.

VERONYKA: Nope. We spent so much money getting this all together. We can't waste it.

JACK nods, a silent moment between the two.

You got a piece of gum?

JACK: *(a joke)* I do.

> *VERONYKA rolls her eyes. Smiling.*

> *He begins withdrawing a pack of gum from his jacket. Stops.*

Spearmint okay?

VERONYKA: I do too.

> *They throw handfuls of confetti in the air.*

> *She takes his hand, brushes some confetti off it and then holds it.*

> *They stare at each other.*

> *They break apart.*

We dance all night.

JACK: I drink so much, I can barely see by the end. Someone loads Veronyka and me into the cab and takes us home. Sitting in the car. I watch the lights from the buildings fly by. Condo after condo. Lights in the windows. People in the lights. Lives in the people. That's going to be us.

> *VERONYKA sucks a bit of drool back into her mouth without waking up.*

〜

JACK: Surplus value. What is it?

VERONYKA: Surplus value is the difference between the production cost and the price of a commodity. You set out to create and distribute bread. The production cost is a dollar—wheat, water, gas for the oven, etc. You sell it for $1.50. Your labour has taken raw materials, created a finished good, and in the process added $0.50 worth of value. If you are a lone baker, you pocket that $0.50 difference between the production cost and price.

JACK: But you don't own a bread factory, so you work in one. The owner pays you $15 an hour. You work eight hours a day. In that day, you make 1,200 loaves of bread—or $0.10 a loaf. But the bread still sells for a $1.50, meaning the owner pockets $0.40 for every loaf. That $0.40—the difference between the price and the production cost, which now includes your labour—is the surplus value. Where does it come from? The labour of the worker. Where does it go now? The owner.

Now flip your perspective—imagine that you're an owner of a bread factory. You sell your bread for $1.50, with a surplus value of $0.40. Then another factory owner starts to charge $1.45 for the same product. Customers move to them and your bread is rotting on the shelves. You can take your prices down to $1.45 or even $1.40 in order to remain competitive but then you're going to extract less surplus value. To maintain that $0.40 per loaf—which is what your standard of living and the growth of your business is based on—money has to be squeezed out somewhere. One way to extract more money is to drive down costs of production. One way to drive down cost of production is to reduce labour costs.

VERONYKA: One way to decrease labour costs in a non-unionized space is to switch from time wages to piece wages. The effects of which we will look at later.

~~~

JACK: So we are freshly married.

They flash their rings.

And we never see each other.

VERONYKA: There are 168 hours in a week. I spend 40 at job one.

JACK: I work 16 hours, four days a week.

VERONYKA: I spend 22 at job two,

JACK: My "weekend" involves me only working 8 hours on the other three days, so that's 88 hours minimum.

VERONYKA: After working two jobs I need 8 hours of sleep a night. So that's 118 of my 168 hours. Add 15 hours a week on transit, which is probably more like 20, and we're at 133 hours a week.

JACK: I'm at 140 of my 168 hours.

VERONYKA: Add the hours a week shopping for food, preparing it and eating it and I'm at 150. Plus laundry.

JACK: Personal hygiene.

VERONYKA: And all the fucking little errands.

JACK: So the little time we have, we spend together.

VERONYKA: Often sleeping.

JACK: We end our Saturday nights together. I bring her back to her place—

VERONYKA: Our place.

JACK: Yeah . . . yeah. Our place. I take her back to our place and we crawl into bed and generally fall right to sleep. Since I don't have to work till 3:00 p.m. on Sunday and since she doesn't have to work at all we don't set alarms. It feels so good to not set an alarm. It makes me feel like I'm in charge of my own life. Just lying in bed because we want to lie in bed. There's no feeling like it in the whole world.

VERONYKA: Three or so hours pass like that. Sometimes we kiss or fuck. Sometimes we don't. Sometimes we listen to the birds singing outside and slide back and forth between sleeping and waking. At 1:00 I call my mom.

JACK: When she calls her mom I dig out an econ book. I'm gonna go back to school again soon. Ma had a few health scares in my final semester, and I was so stressed I failed most of my midterms. I dropped out to avoid ruining my GPA.

It's just five classes, I can get it done. Maybe night school, maybe part time. I stash away little bits of money here and there. I call it the future fund.

VERONYKA: It's a little hard to talk to my mom sometimes. There's never a lot of news. A few names of old friends of hers that have died. Complaints about her knees. Dmitri is still in university, he's still seeing Katya, they're still hoping to get married, Dad is still drinking too much and brooding too much. Dmitri and I have a plan. I keep a roof over Mom and Dad's head while Dmitri is in school. Once he graduates he can take care of them and I can save for their retirement. $30,000 Canadian is enough for the rest of their lives in Chişinău. With hard work I can do this in two or three years . . . Or maybe, four or five . . . or—it doesn't matter. I will do it and then I will be free.

JACK: I get an email from the New Democrats. It's titled, "It's not too late to build a better world." They're gathering volunteers for the next election. I think about it for a while. I like the NDP and I liked working on their campaigns in college. They're thrilling in a really dorky way. But that would cut into my peaceful mornings with Veronyka.

VERONYKA: Ебать! Чертовы тупые ублюдки. Лживые ебаные пизды. *(Schas po ebalu poluchit, suka bliad.)* [*Fuck! Fucking stupid motherfuckers. Lying fucking cunts.*]

JACK: Hey. Heyheyhey. What's going on?

VERONYKA: That lying fucking grocer down the street. I say, "Is this going to be okay till tomorrow?" and he said, "It'll be perfect just like you." Fucking pig. And now look at this. Look at this! Moldy. Rancid fucking avocado.

JACK: Aw shit . . .

VERONYKA: I've been looking forward to a nice meal all week. Might as well just put the money down the drain for all the good it does.

JACK: It's okay. Lunch's going to be great.

VERONYKA: Waste, a fucking waste of time and money trying to do something nice. Everyone's out to fuck you over and they all get away with it.

> *JACK takes her hand. He runs his finger across it taking some of the avocado off. He eats it.*

JACK: Delicious.

> *VERONYKA looks at him for a minute and then laughs a little through her anger.*

VERONYKA: You like it? You want some more?

JACK: Oh, no. No thanks!

VERONYKA: Come on, just a taste.

> *She is jokingly menacing him with the handful of smushed avocado.*

JACK: No, I'm good. I'm full.

VERONYKA: Just a little nibble!

JACK: Stay away! Stay away from me!

> *She lunges for him. They wrestle and goof around trying to smush the avocado flesh into each other.*

> *They both end of on the floor with avocado on their faces and clothes. Happy sigh.*

Shit. We should probably clean this up.

VERONYKA: Yeah, probably.

> *She licks a bit of avocado off his face. He grabs her arm and kisses her.*

> *They break off. She laughs.*

Take me now, amidst the avocados.

JACK: I like the sound of that.

VERONYKA: Mmmm.

JACK: And I was thinking...

> *He kisses her.*

Given that we're wed,

> *He kisses her again.*

And given that we're so so happy,

> *He kisses her again.*

Maybe we forget the condom. See if anything... develops.

VERONYKA: No.

Beat

JACK: Uhh . . . okay. Wh—?

VERONYKA: We have so much family already. How do we pay for diapers, and more mouths, and daycare? And we raise them in this place?

JACK: It doesn't have to be here or now, but I would like to . . . later . . . think about it at least . . .

VERONYKA: Jack . . .

JACK: Forget I said anything. We can think about it down the road . . . in a couple of years.

VERONYKA: Uhh . . . okay . . . maybe.

Neither of them believe this maybe.

Beat.

Jack. Jack. Look at me. I love you. You're enough for me. I don't need more family. I have you.

JACK: Okay.

Beat.

I love you, too.

We don't talk about it again. We focus on each other. On being enough for each other.

VERONYKA: I quit the factory because it's shit. I ask for a pay raise at the Kilt now that I'm legal and they fire me. I get two new serving jobs downtown because that's where best tips are.

JACK: We move out of Veronyka's apartment. I thought it made more sense to stay here but Veronyka insists. We find something similar in a different part of Etobicoke. I have $900 less a month than when I lived with Ma and Ba.

VERONYKA: I'm making almost $1000 more a month, but now I'm also paying tax on my wage and declaring my tips. I pay Vlad one last time. He says he'll miss me. I hope he fucking rots.

JACK: I have almost $30,000 left on my student loans, so I pay $363 a month there. I squirrel away whatever is left at the end of the month to the future fund.

VERONYKA: Anything I have leftover I save for my parents.

JACK: I register for a night class next semester.

VERONYKA: Christmas.

JACK: My parents are very good people and decide to do something really nice at Christmas.

VERONYKA: His parents didn't tell us that they were doing this.

JACK: They suggested in the fall that they might.

VERONYKA: They must have said it in Chinese.

JACK: They asked about how your grandmother was doing, they asked if your parents would be able to leave her for a few days.

She glares at him for a moment before sighing and looking away.

VERONYKA: I remember the conversation now. Jack's right. I was just . . . so tired it didn't really connect as real thing that could really happen. They want to meet my parents and so they bought them plane tickets.

JACK: Which was a very nice gesture but not one they can really afford.

VERONYKA: And one that my parents can't really afford.

JACK: Well—

VERONYKA: And one that we can't really afford.

JACK: Ba's been getting a bonus every Christmas since he got his taxi license. He found two round trip tickets from Moldova for $2,000 and bought them on credit. He figures the bonus will cover most of it. He says "it's a wedding present."

VERONYKA: Jack, I don't want my parents to come here.

JACK: We'll manage.

VERONYKA: You cannot understand. Moldova is dirt poor.

JACK: I know what it's like to be poor.

VERONYKA: You know here. This is different. My parents skip one meal a week so they have something for the offering plate. One coffee will cost them one day's wages, one night hotel will cost them one month.

JACK: That's crazy.

VERONYKA: That is my life. If Ba wants to give us a wedding present, he can send us to Moldova. My parents cannot afford to come here. Ba has to return the tickets.

JACK: "Return them? I can't return them. I didn't get the . . . (. . .) the y'know the

(in Cantonese) 機票取消保險 *(Jīpiào qǔxiāo bǎoxiǎn.)*

(in English) Cancellation insurance." "Why didn't you get the cancellation insurance" "Why would they cancel?" He was trying to save money, and the cancellation insurance costs extra.

VERONYKA: So they're coming. Jack's parents have two bedrooms, we have one. He says all the parents will stay together. This is not a good idea. None of this is a good idea.

JACK: Ba gets his Christmas bonus. It's $300. I empty out the future fund so he's not killed by the interest. I drop my night class but I only get a 50% refund. Still, I need the hours back. It'll mean putting off college, and . . . the future. But it's fine. "I'm sorry. I will make it up to you. We will come together as one family, you, us, Veronyka, her parents. One family. One. This will be worth it."

Veronyka can't get off work, so I pick up her parents at the airport. The flight is three hours late, and I didn't pack lunch. I go to Tim's—a bagel, a coffee, a donut, and a bagel, and a donut: $5.89 and settle in at the gate to wait.

VERONYKA: I'm on lunch break, tapping and staring at my phone waiting for the call. Verushka. Verushka. My child. She is crying. I'm crying. When will I see you. He is so handsome. You love him? I love him, Mom. When we will I see you? Soon, Mom, yes, y— You will have such beautiful children—I try and say, "How was your flight?" But I just say, "your flight?" over and over.

Beat.

Every time we go to Jack's parents place I end up sleeping the whole way home in a coma of crispy pork but this meal surpasses all others. My parents bring a bottle of Russian vodka as a gift. We toast together with Russian vodka and Jack's dad's horrible rum. It's madness. I'm translating my mother's Russian and helping my dad out whenever he doesn't know a word so that Jack can translate it into Chinese and everyone just keeps answering every question with two more questions and a shot of terrible liquor and so the whole thing is just laughing and red faces and a roar of confusing languages. At one point my dad says that he was stationed in the Far East in the '80s when he was an army engineer and he learned one phrase in Chinese, a toast for special occasions. He says it aloud.

JACK: It literally means, "I'm a dumb Russian who shits himself."

VERONYKA: As if it isn't hard enough to hear Jack say it without losing it, I have to then repeat it in Russian. My mother wants to make sure my father hasn't done something to offend our host. I'm drunk, I just blurt it out. My father thinks this is hysterical. He keeps saying it.

It is surprising. It is . . . a nice night.

JACK: Then Ba says:

(drunk) "You're a good man, Marius. A very good man. I have a proposition for you. A business deal."

VERONYKA: And Dad says, "Business. Is always this way with Chinaman."

JACK: Ba laughs. He thinks this is hilarious.

VERONYKA: I can hear the tone shift in my father's voice. No one else can but I can.

JACK: "My son told me you work in the government. I'm just a cab driver and my wife doesn't work anymore. We're not rich. But I'm reliable. We need these kids to get ahead. A better life than ours. I want us to buy them a house with a little yard for the grandchildren."

VERONYKA: Please stop talking, please stop talking.

JACK: "We can get them a starter home for half a million. We will pay the mortgage, condo fees, and taxes. We'll find a way. We only need the down payment. $25,000. We paid for the wedding, and your tickets here. I know this is not equal, but I think it is fair, maybe."

VERONYKA: "Veronyka, is he asking me for money?" It's . . . a joke. It's just a joke. "Does he think I'm rich?"

JACK: This was Ba's plan. This is why he bought the tickets.

VERONYKA: "They're expecting something? They're putting on this little feast, giving us these tickets. Just so they could shake us down for money?"

VERONYKA: No, no. I— When Jack and I got married we gave his parents money. We said it was from you. We told him you and Mom had some money.

JACK: Cristina is pulling Marius's sleeve. Ama asks if Ba said something inappropriate.

VERONYKA: "You told me they paid for the wedding. I didn't ask for this trip. I didn't ask for you to get married. I especially didn't tell you to marry one of these people."

JACK: Marius, Ba doesn't know what he's talking about. Forget he said anything.

VERONYKA: "Poor, I am poor because my country is poor. My country is made poor, it is made into the toilet of Europe, so that your country can be rich. Why don't you go back to rice paddies and I'll stay here and then we'll see who is a man. Then we'll see who can take care of our children."

JACK: And his fist goes through the wall.

VERONYKA: Mom and Dad stay at our house for the rest of the "vacation." I sleep on the couch, Jack stays with his parents. Dad doesn't leave the bedroom, and I don't speak to him for the rest of the trip. His brooding, his anger, it is driving me crazy. I am shaking at work every day. I knew this would happen! I told Jack.

I call in sick on the last day and take Mom downtown. We go to Pusateri's, and Mom says something that's so funny, "This looks like the posters from my childhood." I splurge and buy us cappuccinos.

Mom takes the paper napkin from the café as a souvenir, she folds it just so, and places it in her purse. Jack takes them to the airport the next day.

JACK: Ba's mad at me for lying and making him embarrass himself. I'm mad at him for coming up with this dumb scheme of his. Marius and Cristina are mad at our whole country but especially Ba. Veronyka and I are mad at each other about . . . I don't know. About who our families are? About who we are?

(to VERONYKA) I'm going to get involved in the election campaign.

VERONYKA: Like . . . running?

JACK: No, no. Just volunteering.
I'll lose a few hours a week but nothing we can't handle.
We can't donate so this is the next best thing.

VERONYKA: No.

JACK: What?

VERONYKA: The budget I've made is based on you working a consistent number of hours a week. I'd love to work less but everything's too tight.

JACK: But getting involved in the process is how we improve things for ourselves.

VERONYKA: Mmmm. You make yourself a politician friend who might be able to help us out. Get you a good job. Yes, okay. This makes sense. Good to know someone in government.

JACK: Well,

(laughs) I don't know if we're going to Queen's Park. This riding will go Liberal or Conservative . . . but we'll bring a lot of interesting conversations to the debate and—who knows? The groundwork of this election will pay off in the next.

VERONYKA: No, I don't understand again. Would you be working for the losing candidate? Why would you do that? The loser has as much power as you do.

JACK: They align with . . . y'know . . . my beliefs.

VERONYKA: And the winners don't?

JACK: Yeah, on some things—but not on everything.

VERONYKA: On enough?

JACK: I don't want to think of politics like that.

VERONYKA: You want to work less. Okay, not fair to me but okay, you're going to make a friend in government who will help us, this makes sense to me. It's an investment.

JACK: I just . . . I think the NDP will make the kind of changes I want.

VERONYKA: Will they be elected?

JACK: No.

VERONYKA: Then they won't make the changes you want.

JACK: *(to the audience)* I went to school with the president of the Young New Democrats, Harjeet. We worked on an NDP election campaign together. When he graduated he got himself a job with the Liberals. He wanted a career and the NDP couldn't give him one.

Plus I do like the Liberal candidate. He's progressive enough to run for the NDP but he's obviously done the same math as Harjeet . . . and Veronyka . . . and me, I guess.

I start working for the Liberal campaign in Etobicoke. I have even less time than ever before but it feels good to be doing something, to be knocking on doors and stuffing envelopes. To be part of a great big machine all pointed towards election day.

VERONYKA: *(as Mai, Liberal Campaign Manager, until noted)* What do you mean they're— No, Sandra, I understand what the words "we can't find him" mean when arranged in that order. What I mean is, "Why the fuck can't you find him?" When your job is to find him, is to have him with you. To run through the opening remarks with him. To go over what the candidate will be saying. To make sure he doesn't have a fucking lisp. All of those things you're supposed to be doing. I wasn't asking for a definition of "We" "Can't" "Find" or "Him." I was asking why you're called the volunteer coordinator when your volunteers are always so fucking uncoordinated.

> *Exhales through gritted teeth.*

I'm sorry Sandra. That was unnecessary. Do we have a replacement for him . . . fuck. Do we have anyone who can do this? . . . There's no time . . . He's at Mitzie's thing in Scarborough . . . I—give me a second.

(to JACK) Hey, you at the phone there. Are you Chine— Uh. Hi! I'm Mai, I'm the campaign manager. Really pleased to meet you. The

volunteers are the real backbone of any campaign, so a big thank you to you. Can I ask you something?

JACK: Course.

VERONYKA: Umm . . . are you, by chance Chinese?

JACK: I am . . .

VERONYKA: Do you speak Cantonese?

JACK: 這是我的第一語言 *(Zhè shì wǒ de dì yī yǔyán.) [It's my first language.]*

VERONYKA: *(into the phone)* I have a bad idea. I'll text you.

    She hangs up.

Do you have plans for the next two hours?

JACK: I was going to keep phoning people for the next half hour, and then go and hit the five o'clock rush.

VERONYKA: Could you do us a favour?

I'm going to a rally in East Chinatown for our Toronto–Danforth candidate and we were supposed to have the introduction of our guy happen in Cantonese but they've come down with a stomach flu or something.

JACK: I— Ummm . . . when?

VERONYKA: Five minutes ago.

Beat.

JACK: I'm sorry, I have to pick up more fares tonight. I haven't hit my daily earnings.

VERONYKA: Okay, what if we gave you—

Does some quick math.

Two hundred dollars.

JACK: So we hop in my cab and take off for East Chinatown.

VERONYKA: Do you know anything about the Liberals' "Caring for Hard Working Ontarians" tax plan?

JACK: It's a two-pronged effort to drive small business creation in squeezed-out areas. You— We are promising to decrease the middle bracket of income tax and the small business tax by one percentage point each and providing means-tested exemptions to the employer health tax in designated revitalization zones.

VERONYKA: Don't get into the tax brackets, people don't understand them. Just say "tax on the middle class." Can you walk me through how it affects folks at Gerrard and Broadview?

JACK: Not a lot of middle class at Gerrard and Broadview. Especially among the Chinese community. It's a pretty working-class area.

VERONYKA: We use the term Middle Class and Those Working Hard to Join It. Please make sure you do as well whenever you're speaking on behalf of the party. No one says "working class" anymore.

JACK: Well, what traditionally defines "middle class"? Two-car garage, nuclear family, retirement package, nine to five. That's not East Chinatown. All those folks moved to Markham and Richmond Hill as soon as they could.

VERONYKA: We're going to meet the small business owners who built this community.

JACK: Look, I'm not going to tell you how to do your job. I can translate the words "middle class." I just think it's an odd choice of language.

VERONYKA: None of the parties say working class anymore. You say working class and you're knocking people down the ladder. It's dispiriting.

JACK: But how many people are already down there?

VERONYKA: Oh, most of them. No question. But we're talking about people's lives. Sometimes the idea that they're doing well is enough. So: The Caring for Hard Working Ontarians tax plan.

JACK: Right! So you give tax breaks to Pearl Court Dim Sum and New Valley Flower, as well as income tax breaks to the owners. So then they give their employees a raise, who spend that money at local businesses. Increase the velocity of money, more dollars in everyone's pocket.

VERONYKA: That's perfect.

JACK: But aren't the small business owners just going to pocket the tax cut and not raise the wages?

VERONYKA: They're absolutely going to, but when they donate to the party, we can win, then we can work with them on the minimum wage or on— Oh, shit we're way off track. Okay so you go in, you say, "Ni hao je m'appelle . . . "

JACK: Jack.

VERONYKA: Okay, this is Jack Layton's old riding, it's probably best to downplay any Jack related (. . .). Do you have another name you could go by tonight?

JACK: . . . Ding Heung

VERONYKA: Dan-jang. Perfect. You're one of the people.

JACK: I guess I am.

Three different women who might have been Ma give me dumplings. One woman complains to me about how the city never sweeps her street. An old man tells me about how his building got bought out by a management company and they're trying to double his rent. I meet the candidate afterwards. Charming as hell. Says I can be a volunteer coordinator for the coming federal election in November. He says the Markham seat's winnable, but we need a volunteer coordinator who is fluent in Canto. And best of all it comes with a bit of money. Not nearly minimum wage when I consider the number of hours they're talking about but it's closer to the centre. Closer to the real power.

VERONYKA: *(as herself)* Jack.

JACK: What happened?

VERONYKA: Ba was going to the pharmacy to fill Ma's prescriptions, jumped the curb and crashed into hydro pole. The car is finished.

JACK: He's shaking and crying when I get to the hospital. He's all banged up. They shine the light in his eyes, and . . .

VERONYKA: The doctors call it macular degeneration. It starts as light sensitivity, a little blurring, trouble with colours. Unnoticeable at first.

JACK: But then it accelerates. And for the last couple months, he's been developing a blind spot in his field of vision. They can slow its progress with some shots, but the blind spot will keep getting bigger.

VERONYKA: Ba! You're lucky you didn't kill someone!

JACK: *(as Ba)* They would have taken my license. No licence, no work. No work—

VERONYKA: They do take his license. Obviously.

JACK: They have no income. Their combined pension is about $23,000 a year.

VERONYKA: You have to sell the taxi plate, drive Uber.

You said what kept you there was your father's stupid idea that Uber was a fad. We'll never pay off the loan if the taxi's not operating twenty-four hours.

JACK: I can't.

VERONYKA: Why not?

〜
〜

JACK: There are lots of reasons not to work for Uber, not to work in the gig economy. One of them is piece wages. Jack isn't thinking about the difference between what piece wages and hourly wages do structurally. If he were he might have more to say to Veronyka.

VERONYKA: Time wages compensate you for your time, like with an hourly wage or yearly salary. Think back to the factory where you're paid $15 an hour for eight hours, and your wage works out to $0.10 a loaf. What if your wage was $0.10 a loaf, full stop—no wage for the time you're in the bathroom, on lunch, talking to your co-workers. You're not paid for the amount of time you put in, you're paid for the number of pieces you produce. More bread, more bread. That is the piece wage.

JACK: The whole cab industry is pieces—fares—

VERONYKA: And most of the serving industry is pieces—tips.

JACK: The piece wages mean workers can make a little more money by working harder, and the owners maintain surplus value by losing unproductive workers.

VERONYKA: Now zoom out. Remember how profit is produced? If multiple owners paying piece wages start competing, surplus value will fall. So owners will have to squeeze out money from somewhere if they don't want their standard of living to fall, or their shareholders to complain. One way to squeeze out more money is to reduce the wage per piece produced.

JACK: In the cab industry, workers unionized to set price floors. That meant that the piece wage couldn't keep dropping. In the gig economy, like Uber, that's not an option.

VERONYKA: Now the workers must work harder just to maintain their wage. Now the workers compete with each other, and owners reap the gains.

JACK: So that's part of the 150-year-old theory. Is it useful?

〰

JACK shakes his head.

VERONYKA: One of the bartenders drives Uber in the morning rush. He says he makes bank.

JACK: This taxi was Ba's whole life.

VERONYKA: This is sentimental. You need to decide between his life and yours.

JACK: I won't abandon my parents.

VERONYKA: I'm not asking for this. Every month I'm sending money to my parents. I don't want to abandon anyone. You said that taxi is in the shits. This is a good time to leave it. No?

JACK: That doesn't solve their problem. Ba bought the taxi plate for $150,000, he still has $70,000 left to pay off. The market has collapsed since Uber, we'd be lucky to get half that for selling. Ba's qualified to be a Walmart greeter and that's about it. Ma can't even carry on her old bottle collecting route. I mean it's a good thing my parents live in public housing . . . I have an idea.

VERONYKA: What is it?

JACK: You're not going to like it. What if we moved in with my parents? We could save the rent and use it to service the loan.

VERONYKA: You're right. I don't like it.

Okay. Okay. Okay. Okay. We move into your parents' house. We sell the plate before it's completely worthless. We buy a new car and you drive Uber. We aren't cutting your parents off but no more sentiments. Okay?

JACK: Okay. We rent a moving van to head to Markham.

VERONYKA: I live in a different city now. My last name is Woo now. Vlad doesn't know this. Maybe I'm free of him but I want to be sure. I make a call to the anonymous tip line. I hope he fucking rots.

JACK: I sell the plate to a guy named Mohamed. He was a doctor where he came from, but they won't let him practice here. His whole family put in to get this taxi plate. I feel sick.

We can't handle another loan. No more interest. I find a 2007 Toyota Camry for $3,000 that'll pass the Uber inspection. I empty and close the future fund to buy it. I'm never getting back to school. And kids . . .

    VERONYKA laughs.

VERONYKA: Our schedules become perfect opposites. Jack works every day, I work every night. There are no more Sunday morning wakeups. No more rotten avocado fights. Two kisses a day are hellos and goodbyes.

JACK: I sit in my car, waiting for passengers. In between, I make phone calls for the Liberals, trying to recruit volunteers for the upcoming election. For weeks or months, it seems that life is only about waiting. Waiting for a passenger. Waiting for a someone to pick up the phone.

VERONYKA: Waiting for work to begin. Waiting for work to end.

JACK: Waiting.

Beat.

VERONYKA: And waiting.

Pause.

JACK: And waiting.

Silence.

VERONYKA: His mom has sensitivities to all sorts of medications and the side effects are often just as bad as what they're supposed to be helping. One day I come home and she's on the floor. All around her is broken glass and half-made pot stickers. Ba was at the doctor, Jack was at work. Ma had been on the ground there for two hours. Not in danger or anything but simply not able to get up again. She cries as I lift her to her feet and set her in a chair. She can't stop saying sorry. "For being heavy." She doesn't have the words in English.

JACK: 包袱，一種負擔。 *(Bāofú.)* A burden.

VERONYKA: Now I do the cooking too.

(to JACK) I don't know how to make what your parents like.

JACK: You can learn.

VERONYKA: Why don't you learn?

JACK: I'm driving.

VERONYKA: Why can't your dad cook, he's home enough.

JACK: He's half blind!

VERONYKA: He doesn't know how to cook and refuses to learn. Admit it.

JACK: Would you like to try and make him?

VERONYKA: I go through the grocery list and cost everything I can. I won't even be able to make it work at No Frills. I end up going to Chinatown like Jack had suggested. I grab a pork shoulder. There's so much food here it's falling off the shelves.

I remember drought when I was young. Bad harvests. All Moldovan farmers sold what they had to Romanians and Hungarians. Supply low, demand high. They were hungry too, but they had more money. All our shops were empty. Then Uncle Vadim called the whole neighborhood to his butcher shop, and there was this enormous cow on the table. No one knew how he got it.

JACK: There is the magic of free enterprise.

VERONYKA: He was laughing and talking to the crowd, giving them a show. He had given the cow the name, Khrushchev because he was (. . .) like Khrushchev. Face like this (. . .). You know, big wart. He kept making it bang its hoof on the counter. Making the little children laugh. He had it open down the middle and was reaching in to sever one of the sheets of muscle. His mouth was wide with his impression of Khrushchev at the UN saying, "We will bury you," and out of the cow comes this green-white stream of pus. A huge pocket of infection in the cow's muscles. It sprayed like a firehose. Right in his face, in his open mouth. Sprayed like that for a full fifteen seconds. The cow shrivelled to nothing and the room was filled with a terrible smell. Me and everyone else ran fast out of the butcher shop with my uncle roaring, "Rats! Rats! You're all stinking rats! Come back and help me!" He was right. We were rats. So was he. So was his gangster friend and the communists and the capitalists, everyone.

Shift.

I ride the GO home with the pork shoulder, and I think of my mom, stuck in Moldova. Evening, Mom.

JACK: *(as VERONYKA's mom, until noted)* God bless you, Veronyka.

VERONYKA: G'bless you too, Mom.

JACK: How was church today?

VERONYKA: I just came back. The service was very nice.

(to the audience) This is a lie.

JACK: We lit a candle for your name day.

VERONYKA: Thank you, Mom. Jack did too.

JACK: Jack comes with you?

VERONYKA: He did today. He goes with his family to the Chinese Baptist church, remember?

(to the audience) This is also a lie. His folks are, at best, really lazy Buddhists.

VERONYKA: How're you feeling today?

JACK: Good, I have news. I don't know if you'll think it's good news . . . I think it's good news.

VERONYKA: Oh . . . what is it?

JACK: Your brother was offered a job!

VERONYKA: A job? He—what? He has two more years before he's an engineer.

JACK: Yes, to be an engineer. He's impatient though. You know how it is. He was offered a job on a Russian tanker, he's going to take it.

VERONYKA: Are you fucking kidding me?

JACK: Verushka!

VERONYKA: I left my home and you and my whole life just to try and get him an education. He blows it off so he can make quick money.

JACK: He wants to start his life. He gets a job to do this.

VERONYKA: Yeah, working for the fucking Russians.

JACK: He's so excited to start working. Why can't you be happy for him? He's such a special boy.

VERONYKA: Happy for him? I've spent thousands of dollars and he pisses it all away.

JACK: Dmitri needs money now. He has to pay for a wedding and a house. He has to raise a family. He has plans for the future.

VERONYKA: And what about my future?

JACK: Where is your family, Veronyka?

VERONYKA: If I poopped out five kids would your sweet baby Dimonushka finally have to put on his own pants?

If Dmitri isn't going to school anymore then he can pay for you and Dad. That's that.

JACK: You are—you think you're so important now. You're a Canadian now with your car and your apartment and your coffee that costs $100 while your parents starve. You know you might have died without me, Veronyka? How much easier my life would have been if I had just let you go? Apologize this instant!

Silence.

VERONYKA: Mom . . .

JACK hangs up.

VERONYKA is momentarily overpowered by rage. She throws her phone across the room.

She gets a good hold of the pig carcass, raises her cleaver up, and brings it down with immense force on a tendon easily severing it.

This meat is shit. I do what I can. I peel away layers of sinew and muscle. I try and reveal what is wholesome, tender, worthy. There is so little to show for the effort. Beggars can't be choosers.

JACK: *(as himself)* My parents aren't beggars.

VERONYKA: They're living off pathetic old age security and our kindness.

JACK: That doesn't make them beggars.

VERONYKA: What does it make them then?

JACK: *(a little acid)* Family.

The federal election is on. It's a long one. Markham–Stouffville is the conservative heartland, but we're only down by four points right now. If we can scare NDP voters with the spectre of a Tory victory we can maybe win this one.

Our candidate is Mai. She was the one who I took to the rally all those months ago. The party brass has decided to give her a chance to run for the Markham seat. Her husband is her campaign manager. He's this dumpy ex-bureaucrat, but he's organized. It's eighty-eight hours a week, plus as many hours as I can drive for Uber, but honestly, I'm happy to be out of the house.

VERONYKA: I'm downtown Monday afternoon to pick up my cheque from the restaurant and I'm passing through Chinatown and there's a sale on poultry. The window is full of skinny chickens, once pink but now they are the colour of sidewalk. I buy one of them. I save $3.00 off the Markham price. I am thrilled at the savings. I'm disgusted at how thrilled I am.

On the way home I decide to stop in Kensington Market. The difference of a block, but it's a world away. Everyone is speaking English, punks drinking the tall cans and hippies smoking pot, all the Rosedale bitches in summer hats. I go into the butcher shop there. It's so clean, the chickens in the coolers have skin that looks an inch thick.

Where do you get these chickens?

JACK: *(as the butcher, until noted)* We have relationships with farms north of Barrie and east of Guelph. They're all pasture-raised.

VERONYKA: He shows me pictures. It's stupidly romantic. Little farms, trees, goats.

JACK: And the beef is from heritage breeds, humanely raised, and hormone-free from near Uxbridge and Simcoe. Local tastes better. Do you work in the industry?

VERONYKA: In restaurant. My uncle was a butcher.

JACK: No kidding. Are you gonna pick up the family trade?

VERONYKA: I've thought about it.

JACK: Maybe our ham will convince you.

VERONYKA: Oh, this is a little out of my price range.

JACK: But you just paid for it.

VERONYKA: I'm not wearing my ring. I took it off when I was cooking last night and . . . forgot to put it back on. And then he gives me a ham sandwich. It's innocent, obviously. But Jesus, this is incredible.

Best meal I've had since I came to Canada. I'm so fucking fed up with Chinese food.

JACK: I'm going to close up early. Do you want to have a beer? On me.

VERONYKA: I know I should go home. It's a hot day and it's going to be a hot ride home for this uncooked bird. I haven't had a beer in months, doesn't fit in the budget.

(to the butcher) On you? Sure.

VERONYKA: One beer turns into three as we sit and chat. It's so free and easy. He's smart and funny and he's got a plan. He's opening another shop next week. He's going to need butchers, he'd be willing to train me.

JACK: Maybe you can open your own shop in Markham someday. It feels good to be the boss.

VERONYKA: I watch the condensation gather on the fresh round of beer that he promises will be our last before he takes me home. I watch the condensation gather on the inside of the bag of chicken. I promise it'll be my last.

~~~

JACK: Marx offers a theoretical framework for examining relations between owners and workers, but do 19th century theories measure up to 21st century reality? What does the data say?

VERONYKA: Thomas Piketty analyzed two hundred years of data, and despite having never read Marx and admitting that he had no intention to, came to a somewhat similar conclusion. He found that there's a central dynamic in capitalism, and that is that the rate of return on capital, in terms of investments, dividends, profits, and rents (or r) is consistently greater than the growth of wages and salaries (g).

VERONYKA writes r>g on the board.

JACK: r in Piketty's model is similar to MCM in Marx, the exchange form for owners; r represents all the ways owners extract money: owning a factory or shares in Uber, being a landlord, while g is like the CMC form, for Veronyka and Jack who exchange their labour for wages. If r grows faster than g, on aggregate money from capital will have better returns than money from labour. This means inequality between owners and workers—owners having capital, workers having labour—will always grow.

VERONYKA: Of all the wealth created in 2017, 82% of it was captured by the 1%, while 3.7 billion people, half the world, didn't see any new wealth. Let's say that one more time.

Of all the wealth created in 2017,

JACK: 16.7 trillion dollars

VERONYKA: 82% of it

JACK: 13.7 trillion dollars!

VERONYKA: Was captured by the 1%, while 3.7 billion people, half the world, didn't see any new wealth. Societies with most social mobility between classes—Jack and Veronyka "getting ahead"—are the societies with the least inequality. It's easier to travel between classes when the classes are closer together. The bottom group can "get ahead" through either strong labour unions who bargain for better wages, or governments who redistribute wealth, primarily through free post-secondary education, free health care, and public housing.

JACK: To facilitate social mobility, Piketty suggests a financial speculation tax, a global tax on wealth, and a return to pre-Reagan and Thatcher income tax levels—up to 90% on the super wealthy.

VERONYKA: He also admits this is impossible because politics is dominated by those who hold that money he'd like to redistribute.

~~~

The butcher drops me off near home. He tells me to come by the shop, if I have the skills there is a position for me. I stare up at the apartment for a long time. I wonder if I would lose my residency if I left them. If I got a divorce. Maybe I could marry this fucking butcher. I want to be on the top of something instead of the bottom.

I prepare the chicken. I don't eat it. I remember the taste of the ham sandwich and I pretend I'm still eating that.

JACK: *(as himself) Clostridium perfringens.*

VERONYKA: Food poisoning.

JACK: I wake up in the middle of the night, I need to vomit, now. I am up and out of bed and running for the toilet. Ma and Ba are already there. Ba lying on the ground beside the tub gasping for breath. Ma collapsed against the toilet. She is covered with vomit. I have one second to register all this before wheeling around and heading for the kitchen. I start to vomit on the way, I have my hands up to my mouth and I catch handfuls of it, thin, yellow streams, with chunks of mostly-chewed chicken. I crash into the sink and heave.

VERONYKA: Ba, what happened?

JACK: "I carried her here. Dropped her. Fell down."

VERONYKA: Ma is crying, she thinks she broke something. She needs an ambulance. She reminds me of a dog my father hit with his car. It shivered and moaned and its eyes were huge and black and terrified. I give Ma a glass of water. If this happened to my mother, who would be there for her?

I drive me and Jack to the hospital. He goes back behind the wall to talk to the doctors. I sit in the waiting room. I chew my cheeks. I wonder if I did it deliberately. I text Jack, "Hey, when you have minute can you come back to the waiting room . . . and hug me?"

JACK: "Pretty busy."

VERONYKA: When he finally decides to come back it's close to five in the morning. I'd been sitting there for four hours.

JACK: Hey . . .

VERONYKA: How are they?

JACK: They're both staying overnight. Ma's being x-rayed right now and Ba's asleep. I'm going to stick around in case Ma needs me. You can go home if you want. I'm okay.

VERONYKA: Okay, are you sure? I'll . . . head home then.

JACK: Okay.

They both face the audience, breaking out of the scene.

BOTH: I love you. I love you. I love you. I love you. You didn't do anything wrong.
You're wonderful.
It's going to be okay.
I'll be just a text away if you need anything.
Are you okay?
Are we okay?
I love you.

They both face back in.

Silence.

VERONYKA: Okay. Bye.

JACK: Bye.

VERONYKA: On my way home, outside of a bar I see this truly enormous splat of vomit. This is recreational vomit. This is the vomit of people who are so healthy and wealthy and bored that they make themselves ill to give themselves something to do. I'm done being paid garbage to serve people till they do this. New plan, find a bus. Go home. Grab a couple hours sleep. Go down to the butcher shop. Tell him I will start today.

JACK: They finish scanning Ma and roll her up beside me.

VERONYKA *(as Ma, until noted)* Jack?

JACK: Yes, Mom.

VERONYKA: It's broken. I can feel it.

JACK: We haven't even seen the x-ray, Ma. Maybe it's just a bad bruise.

VERONYKA: We're going to have to move . . . there are too many stairs. We have to move somewhere else . . . everywhere we go is . . . going to cost so much. And I'll just die anyway.

JACK: Mom!

VERONYKA: Then I'll die and you'll be paying . . . so much more . . . for what? For me? No Jack . . . No.

JACK: One day at a time, Mom.

VERONYKA: For how many days, Jack?

JACK: Ma . . .

> *Beat.*

The doctor says we need to replace Ma's broken hip but that she's frail. Very frail. With her heart condition, her morphine sensitivity, her low white blood cell count. She needs to go home and get stronger before the surgery. We need a wheelchair.

VERONYKA: *(as herself)* Rental $95 a month.

JACK: A commode chair.

VERONYKA: $215.55. Rental not available . . . for obvious reasons.

JACK: A personal support worker

VERONYKA: $600 a week.

VERONYKA: While they meet with the doctor I'm at the butcher shop stuffing pork into sausage casing. I am fucking up, but the butcher is patient. I'm not wearing my ring.

JACK: An ambulance takes Ama back to the house. Two EMTs earn their paychecks carrying her up three flights of stairs as gently and carefully as a newborn. They settle her into her bed. Ba says we'll buy one of those lift beds.

VERONYKA: $1,600.

JACK: She doesn't seem to care. She says she's tired, wants to sleep. She asks me . . . She asks me to take the lid off the bottle of OxyContin in case she needs one in the night. I do. I leave the lid off.

VERONYKA: A friend of mine in Chişinău got addicted to painkillers after a car accident. They said it felt like being jerked off by angels. Maybe that's how Ma went. With angels' hands all over her.

JACK: Aba teaches me the old funeral traditions. I help him take down the mirrors in the house. We hang a cloth near the doorway. We observe all the old customs. Ba won't get his hair cut for the next forty-nine days, he's always kept it shaved.

VERONYKA: People show up for the funeral. A lot. Everyone from the building. Everyone who came to the wedding and more. Did Ma have this many friends? Where have they been?

JACK: I only get three days off the campaign. I'm never home to see it but Veronyka says Ba does the prayer service by himself in our living room every seven days.

VERONYKA: After the forty-nine days, I stop wearing black. I get a full-time job at the butcher shop, and I put my ring back on. The butcher treats me different. But I will not be here long.

JACK: And I get my hair cut. I ask Aba if he wants to, but he says it doesn't matter. He mostly just putters around the house. Sometimes he sings a little bit, when he doesn't know that we're around, all these old folk songs. This one day . . . I come home from the campaign, Veronyka's out. I make a bit of soup for Aba. He shuffles over to the liquor cabinet.

He's looking for his rum, but his eyes are so fucking bad. I grab it, and he says, "Stay home. Celebrate with me." I ask what we're celebrating. "I talked to the bank today. They said when I go, all my debt goes with me. You'll be free." We start drinking. He tells me about his parents. His dad fighting in the revolution. Growing up during the Great Leap Forward. He was born near Shenzhen, when it was smaller than Barrie. Now it's bigger than New York. He keeps laughing about that. He talks about meeting Mom, their decision to leave the country. He listened to English tapes between fares in his cab, she cooked in a restaurant on Spadina. He says, "I'd had a brother. He died in China, almost ten years before I was born. I was an accident. Happy accident. Happiest accident." He says, "You sold my taxi. You drive for Uber now. You should have made me sell years ago, but you're too nice. You've always been too nice. I wanted you to be successful. Finish school, get a real job. You can still do that, Jack. Don't waste what you have."

VERONYKA: When I get home they are both snoring in their chairs with the empty bottle on the ground at their feet.

JACK: Ba dies a week later.

We do the traditions again. I don't know why I do it, but I don't know what else to do.

VERONYKA: I wear black again.

JACK: I pay for the prayer service at the end of the week. We've done everything we're supposed to.

    Beat.

Veronyka?

VERONYKA: Yeah?

JACK: . . .

VERONYKA: Oh, Jack, come here.

They embrace.

JACK: You know what they both talked about . . . at the end? Money. The expenses. They were so scared. So . . . uncertain. They should have been taken care of. They shouldn't have to think about these things.

VERONYKA: This isn't your fault, Jack. You did your best.

JACK: No. No, I didn't. A good son would have provided. I failed them.

VERONYKA: No. We provided.

JACK: That can't be us. I can't live like they did anymore. I can't . . . die the way they did.

VERONYKA: We're not going to be them. We're not going to let the world fuck with us. Your parents—their debt—it's gone. We can start fresh. We can become free.

JACK: Promise?

VERONYKA: I do. Do you?

JACK: I do.

≋

VERONYKA: Why do owners dominate the political system? Because owners designed the political system. John A. Macdonald said, "We (the state) must protect the rights of minorities, and the rich are always fewer in number than the poor."

JACK: Running for political office requires massive amounts of money—for staff, for space, for advertising—so political parties make promises catering to big donors.

VERONYKA: Elections come down to the two parties who can raise the most money and pay for the most advertisements and outreach. These parties then win government, and use the state to create structural changes that will benefit them and their donors.

JACK: There are simple and effective measures available to all governments to reduce inequality and allow people to get ahead. Unfortunately, these measures mean governments redistributing the gains of productivity growth to workers instead of owners.

VERONYKA: So, owners benefit because the exchange form (MCM) has "surplus value." This surplus value is mostly generated through decreasing worker power, like by using piece wages, busting unions, introducing anti-worker legislation, and moving production offshore.

Rates of return on capital (r) have always exceeded wages (g) so inequality always grows. This is the central dynamic of capitalism. Any attempt to undo this dynamic in the political system is impossible, because the political system is designed by and for owners. Will Jack and Veronyka get ahead? These individual ones, maybe—but zoom out. Can all the Jacks and Veronykas in the world get ahead? No. The dynamic of capitalism doesn't allow that.

♒

JACK: It's the last week of the campaign. I get a call from Mai. She's hammered and needs me to pick her up. She's at a hobby farm just outside of town. I pull into the driveway, and she and this dude are sitting on the porch, making out. He's got his hand under her shirt like they're in high school. I drive her home to her husband.

VERONYKA: I look up the address and find out his name. He's a developer.

JACK: Mai manages the planning department.

VERONYKA: This smells like Chișinău . It's all fucked. Everywhere.

JACK: We grab a coffee before a community meeting the next day.

VERONYKA: *(as MAI)* Jack.

JACK: Yeah?

VERONYKA: About what you saw last night. I expect you won't—

JACK: Nope. Don't worry about it.

VERONYKA: Because you'd sink the campaign. You know that, right?

JACK: I won't say anything.

> *Beat.*

VERONYKA: Great.

JACK: We win federally, but we lose this riding by two hundred votes. We were expected to lose it by about two thousand, so promotions are in order. There's a rumour that I can count on a constituency job in one of the other ridings, but that falls through. Mai's really apologetic about it. She says she'll do what she can to help me out.

> *VERONYKA is butchering a hog throughout.*

> *Important thoughts should be punctuated by cuts into the hog.*

VERONYKA: Dmitri sent me an email yesterday. He's been fired from his job on the tanker, knowing him for being drunk. He's too proud to ask for money but that's what he needs. Katya's threatening to leave him, Mom and Dad are worried about future. Everywhere crisis.

This knife was a gift from Jack. I bought a shitty knife set off Kijiji for my first day as a butcher's apprentice. When I got my full-time position at the shop he bought me this. There is no reason that the handle needs to be maple. No reason they had to polish it and buff it until the beautiful, complicated subtleties are brought to the surface. They did it because if something exists it can be made beautiful.

When I was working seventy hours a week and asleep for most of the rest of the time I had to bury all the best parts of me. The parts of me that are curious about every cell in the human body, the parts of me that appreciate coriander, architecture, football strategy. There was no room. There was no time. Now I am excavating her. Every day. I dig down into these animals, I sever tendons and peel flesh from bones. I reveal myself.

This is a special right for those who succeed. Who we are is made in fire, like the steel in this blade. It is crafted, it is created, it cannot simply be given. If it is given it means nothing. Fighting for our place in the world is what makes us good, what makes us beautiful. Not government bringing in 25,000 refugees. Giving them houses and cars. I paid off Vlad. I worked till I was ready to drop. I made it. I belong here. I have carved myself into this country.

    Her phone rings. JACK brings it to her.

JACK: It's your mom.

VERONYKA: Siri, ignore that call. Siri, block that number.

    Beat.

JACK: I get stuck on the 401 for three hours. Veronyka's got herself a business in the making while I'm driving Uber. What am I providing? What am I bringing to the table? I get a text from Mai—

VERONYKA: *(as MAI, until noted)* I'm running in the Markham by-election, I want you on my team.

JACK: "I have the name recognition, and you know every volunteer in Markham."

BOTH: We've got this one.

JACK: It's nice to feel wanted, but it's what—six weeks of insane hours at basically minimum wage? I look through the videos from my dashcam. I never deleted the footage from the hobby farm.

VERONYKA: Jack!

JACK: Mai.

VERONYKA: Are you excited for the announcement?

JACK: That's what I wanted to talk to you about.

VERONYKA: Yeah?

JACK: I want to run.

VERONYKA: What?

JACK: I want to run, for the by-election. I know the community, I've lived here my whole life. People like me. I'm a small business owner.

VERONYKA: You drive for Uber.

JACK: I studied economics in college.

VERONYKA: Then you dropped out.

JACK: I have a relatable narrative. And I want to help people.

VERONYKA: Maybe next time, Jack. It's my turn right now.

JACK: You had yours. You lost. And you have a good job to fall back on, I don't. I need this. It's the fair move.

VERONYKA: The world isn't fair, Jack.

JACK: I know.

> *JACK shows the video on his phone.*

VERONYKA: Jesus Christ.

JACK: I want you to vouch for me in my candidacy.

VERONYKA: You can't be serious.

JACK: We need fresh blood.

> *Beat.*

Mai vouches for me. Her husband becomes my campaign manager. Veronyka and I look great in the photos, I get a bunch of young volunteers. We announce after the long weekend. My campaign manager says, "You're not going to have a day off for the next four months. Anything you have to do, I suggest you do it this weekend."

VERONYKA: *(as herself)* You want to take a vacation?

JACK: I want us to take a vacation.

VERONYKA: I would love that.

We book the long weekend off, and go to Montreal. And I find out that Jack speaks French.

JACK: Un peu.

VERONYKA: It's pretty fucking good.

JACK: D'accord, je suppose.

VERONYKA: And we stay in a hotel in the old town. We go to a spa and to the museum and the concierge at the hotel suggests a nice little restaurant famous for veal. We go and Jack's French comes in handy.

JACK: It's nothing. It's just, the waiter forgot part of Veronyka's order.

VERONYKA: And I brought it up, and the guy said, "Je m'excuse." Like he didn't even care.

JACK: I got kinda mad. We're spending all this money, and the . . . you know, the fucking staff? When was the last time we had a nice meal? "C'est pas acceptable. Où est le manager?" The manager takes our drinks off the bill.

VERONYKA: Which means we can spend the money we had planned to spend on wine on

JACK: More booze!

VERONYKA: We run back to our hotel drunk on each other and have sex like we hadn't had in a long time.

JACK: Veronyka is asleep. I put on a hotel bathrobe and step out onto the balcony. There's a luxury high-rise under construction across the street. I imagine what it'll look like when it's completed.

VERONYKA: I think I dreamed about my mother. The posters from her childhood.

JACK: I imagine the lives that will soon light up these windows. I have never in my life been closer to being one of them.

Acknowledgements

Thank you to Soulpepper Theatre, Tarragon Theatre, and the Ontario Arts Council for funding the development of this piece. Special thank you to the actors who supported and workshopped the play throughout its development: Richard Lam, Susanna Fournier, Amelia Sargisson, Chala Hunter, and Jeff Yung.

Thank you to the team at the Tarragon Theatre: Richard Rose, Andrea Romaldi, and all the others who took this script from a pile and put it on the stage.

Thank you to the creative team for the premiere: Matt Gin, Shannon Currie, Shannon Lea Doyle, Michelle Ramsay, and Kathleen Jones.

Finally, thank you to Guillermo Verdecchia, who has made us better Marxists and playwrights, maybe but not necessarily but probably in that order.

Anthony MacMahon is a Canadian playwright currently working in Toronto. His works include *Animal Farm, The Voyager Concert, The Dead* (Soulpepper), *Trompe la Mort*, and *Wild Dogs on the Moscow Trains* (SummerWorks). He works in progressive politics and in the public service. He's honoured to be an alumni of the Soulpepper Academy, Concordia University, and the University of Saskatchewan.

Thomas McKechnie is a Toronto-based playwright and union organizer. They were a part of the 2013–2015 Soulpepper Academy as a writer. Writing credits include *The Jungle* (Tarragon Theatre, co-written with Anthony MacMahon), *12 Letters from Your Lover*, *Lost at Sea* (with Hannah Kaya), *Worm Moon* (the Theatre Centre's Residency Program), *4 1/2 (ig)noble truths* (zeitpunktheatre/Why Not Theatre, presented in Toronto, Victoria, Vancouver, and more), and *Remembering the Winnipeg General* (ziepunktheatre). They are a founding member of Artists for Climate and Migrant Justice and Indigenous Sovereignty.